HAIKU

Flowers in the Grass
A Collection of Nearly 350 Poems

written by
DALE HANSON

Haiku—Flowers in the Grass by Dale Hanson

Copyright © 2016 Dale Hanson

All rights reserved. No part of this book may be used or reproduced by any means without the written permission of the publisher except in the case of brief quotation embodied in critical articles and reviews.

Cover and author image by Rafe Hanson Photography
Cover and interior design by Jacqueline Cook

ISBN: 978-0-9981353-0-4 (Hardcover)
ISBN: 978-0-9981353-1-1 (e-book)

10 9 8 7 6 5 4 3 2 1

BISAC Subject Headings:
POE025000 POETRY / Haiku
POE023030 POETRY / Subjects & Themes / Nature

Published by Dale Hanson
P.O. Box 2870
Sitka, Alaska 99835

HAIKU

Flowers in the Grass
A Collection of Nearly 350 Poems

written by
DALE HANSON

Contents

Forward vii
Vietnam 9
Virgin Islands 25
Spring...31
Summer 53
Autumn 71
Winter...91
For All Seasons 109
About the Author..155

For all flesh is as grass,
And all the glory of man as the flower of grass.
1 Peter 1:24

Forward

Throughout this book of haiku I have conformed to the centuries-old haiku style of three lines of five, seven, and five syllables. In some other regards, however, I have expanded the boundaries of content.

Some of my haiku are metaphoric — I have also used "like" or "as" in some of the poems. Most of the old masters related their poems to the four seasons, and usually gave "clue" words so the reader would get the connection. The seasons related to the human experience and life around us; birth and beginnings, the prime of life, harvest and maturity, and then ultimately death. Those observations were comparisons and insights to life and in essence were metaphors.

The reader will find some examples of imagery in my poems also. While those poems may challenge the purist definitions of haiku for some readers, I am challenged at times not to share them.

Dale Hanson

I have also placed some narrative before some of the chapters. I have found that the value of many haiku are lost because the poems may have been esoteric and not of the personal experience of the reader. Japanese haiku is an example of this. A dusty doll in a corner of the attic would take on new meaning if one were acquainted with the festival of the dolls.

It is with this in mind that I added a few paragraphs to enhance the poems. They are not stories, but rather verbal photographs.

VIETNAM

I don't see it enter the clearing but there it is: a huge, long white snake about fifty yards downrange of us. We are doing magazine drill, just putting a couple of rounds in each magazine and running through all of our pouches. As it happens, we all finish about the same time. My tribesmen are waiting for my next instruction when we notice the snake. It seems to test the wind — I can see its black tongue flick in and out — and I can imagine the slits in its yellow eyes.

I am a good shot and I am certain I can take its head with a single round. I aim and squeeze one off, but the bullet hits just below and to the front of the snake; I can see the gravel pebbles fly up and a couple of them seem to bounce off the snake's scales. The reflection of the sun on the scales blinks where the pebbles hit.

The snake begins to race across the range left to right, its body stretching forward, head straight out like an arrow.

I take aim again — even leading it a couple of inches — and miss again, and once more pieces of debris strike its side. I have lost any desire now to shoot the snake and I just watch its race to safety on the far side. The snake is white as a target and exposed on the range with distance to go but we track its progress to the edge of the clearing.

The white cobra makes it across the clearing and into the deep brown grass. Only its tail is exposed for a few seconds as if the creature were catching its breath. Then with a flick, the last of the tail disappears, pulling the sun on its scales with it.

* * *

The morning has broken and the Vietnamese workers have lined up at the gate to our camp. The women wear baggy black silk pants and white tops and each has a large conical straw hat on her head. Work passes are clipped to their shirts and they chatter together as they show their passes to the Chinese guards at the gate and then go to their respective work sites.

The fog having lifted, helicopters begin to arrive overhead from Pleiku and settle on the pad. The crews make their way to breakfast at the mess hall.

At the back door of the mess hall a Vietnamese cook in a greasy apron throws out a pail of grey dishwater and it makes the sound of igniting napalm as it hits the ground. The door slams shut on rusty hinges.

Near the gate two small boys have found a

scorpion. They squat over the scorpion and with a short piece of stick they draw a circle around it in the dirt. The scorpion runs along the tiny furrow and seeks an opening in the line. It will not cross the etched line and it seems to desperately seek an opening. It makes the circuit again and finds no escape. The scorpion pauses, stops, and then strikes its own back with its stinger. It writhes about for a minute, shudders, and dies. The children laugh and I can see their teeth are white, not yet stained black with beetle nut. They seem young and innocent of war.

* * *

Outside the wire to the south, Viets are working in the paddies. The paddies smell of feces and stale vegetation. The workers have their pant legs rolled up above their knees and they work in the grey water shoulder to shoulder with each other pushing the rice starts into the mud one at a time.

As we pass, the Viets never look up from their work, as they plant from curfew to curfew.

From the muddy water a large grey water buffalo, the color of the paddy, steps to the raised path. It emerges, taking long smooth strides, not plodding like an ox, but with purpose. I hear the sucking sound as its hoofs leave the mud and a moment of splash as it enters the path.

On the buffalo's back is a tiny boy. He seems to be weightless on the huge beast and he rides as if he's been born to be astride its back. In his hand is a very thin slender stick, much like a wisp of willow.

He touches the animal's shoulder with it and it turns on the path toward the village. Never does the child look at any of us.

* * *

We are just returning from a mission in the Australian sector and they have arranged for us to return to our base in Kontum by a C-119 airplane. In addition to the two of us Special Forces troops, we have six of our Montagnard tribesmen that make up our recon team. In all, the mission wasn't terribly bad, only nerve racking with all of the booby traps and thick jungle. We normally do not encounter booby traps as most of our missions are behind enemy lines — who does that in their own sanctuary?

The Montagnards have their web gear loose; their rifles are slung from their green bandanas. Most have slid their rucksacks up and are dozing with their heads on them.

The plane begins to descend. Suddenly the pilot's maneuvers become sharp and abrupt. The crew chief runs back to us and shouts, "Belt up!" He begins to turn away and then shouts again, "We're taking fire from the ground."

One of the 'yards shuffles over to me and opens his mouth to speak. Just then a piece of shrapnel shoots through the floor and bright white light like a molten dowel rod goes from the opening straight to the 'yard's mouth.

Y Brew's teeth were filed to the gum line as a child so the shrapnel does not hit teeth or bone.

Haiku–Flowers in the Grass

His mouth is already open and the hot metal goes out his left cheek. I'm afraid he could drown in his own blood as it fills his mouth. One of the men pulls an ace bandage from his pouch and begins to wrap it around Y Brew's jaw. Y Brew holds the bandage to his jaw with one hand and never lets go of his weapon with the other.

The crew chief shouts to us again above the noise, "We're taking mortar fire on the field. We're just going to take you to the gate at speed, let you jump off, and then we're taking off." The tailgate drops down and blinding sunlight and oppressive heat fills the plane.

There is a loud, "Kawump!" and we see the impact of a mortar shell as it hits the metal runway and turns it into a metal knot.

As we near the gate the plane does a one-eighty and we jump off the tailgate at a run, Y Brew holding the bandage to his jaw and one of us carrying his rucksack.

A Special Forces Sergeant meets us and we get aboard a three-quarter ton truck for the ride to base.

The shelling isn't accurate and ends with the airplane leaving. One round does hit a building along the road and the impact slams on the tin roof like a freight train door. Twin windows burst outward like a pair of glasses. The shelling appears to be over. People emerge from shelter and wander along the road. At a graveyard nearby, Viets squat behind tombstones of Frenchmen, defecate, and move on.

Dale Hanson

* * *

From the backs of the latrines, men lift hinged wall panels and with large hooks pull out huge rusty tubs the color of excrement. The tubs are made from fifty-gallon fuel drums that have been cut in half. Viet men with kerchiefs around their mouths pour gasoline in the tubs and ignite the contents. The black smoke of the burning is thick — almost too heavy to float in the air.

* * *

Along the perimeter where the Americans quarter, maids do laundry. Mama Sahn washes yesterday's fatigues and hangs them to dry on the rolls of concertina wire that surround the camp. There in the morning sun, uniforms of soldiers, empty of men, lie on their backs with the arms spread out to the sides. One says "Anderson," his sergeant stripes and jump wings become brighter as the uniform dries.

* * *

The commo room is underground in the tactical operations center. There are no windows. There are several radios and from one of them there is a steady static as if a microphone has been keyed. The crackle of the static grows and there is a distant urgent voice calling the commo center.

The sergeant in the commo center leans forward with the microphone in his hand. "Mother Goose, this is Able One!" the voice shouts. It becomes clear that the crackle is not static but heavy gunfire near the speaker. A team of Green Berets is in trouble. They are surrounded deep in enemy territory and there are casualties.

Air support is marshaled to the fight. We listen to the radio traffic and can hear the rifle fire and the thud of grenades in the background and the shouting into the mic.

Jets and helicopters arrive and in the background we can hear explosions and the inhale of napalm as it ignites.

Most of us have gathered our rifles and web gear and are ready in the event they need us on the ground. Our Montagnards are lined up in teams at the helipad, leaning back on their rucksacks waiting for the "Go."

Someone runs up to the pad and quietly says, "They got the team out and they're coming in on strings."

We are all watching to the west. Then very far away we see a dot on the horizon and can hear a very faint rumble of helicopter rotors. The dots come closer and begin to take the shape of helicopters. There are also figures hanging below them by ropes.

The choppers near us and their rumble becomes louder. Now we can see the soldiers who are snapped into the ropes. On the lead chopper we can clearly see a man, Anderson, suspended by rope. The wind catches his fatigues and blows the empty pant legs straight back.

Dale Hanson

* * *

It is dead quiet in the mess hall and we have just been told that in the morning, we will go in where Anderson got it. On the mess hall table is a little sign that says, "Take two salt tablets and drive on."

In the morning as the fog burns off, the choppers can clear the highlands between us and Pleiku. They land to take us to our target. My stomach churns as it does before every mission and I can feel myself keyed up like electricity.

I try to follow the helicopter's route to the target and keep orientated so I know which way to run off the landing zone. As we near the area I can see where the fast movers have strafed and bombed, some of the craters with fresh turned red soil. Around them the trees and jungle are knit together like pick-up-sticks.

The chopper does a split S in the approach and I am challenged to keep orientated. The chopper drops into a clearing and lays the elephant grass down, and we see a huge cobra there. Its hood is flared and its head turns left and right like a periscope.

* * *

The Communists hit our camp three-o-clock Thursday morning. It isn't an important day, really; not Ho Chi Minh's birthday nor an American holiday, nor the anniversary of something. Perhaps that alone makes it a good day for the attack. Leading up to it, everything is routine and quiet.

But some things may have presaged the attack:

Haiku—Flowers in the Grass

It's the start of monsoon season, and you can set your watch by when it rains during the night. At that time of year, the rain begins suddenly and is a heavy downpour — the kind that when under a tin roof of the sentry post you hear nothing else at all. Visibility is gone as well, so sentries would get under cover. The enemy also knows that with the socked-in weather, the camp will not be able to get close air support if it gets hit.

It's Thursday night. A torrent of rain bursts from the darkness and in minutes the cleared area around our camp is water-drenched mud. Through this slick mud, enemy sappers slide through our wire as if weightless. They never trip a flare or tip a noisemaker. Mines are dismantled; claymores cut.

But there is one watchful sentry on guard duty. As he brings a spoon of canned peaches to his mouth, he sees the shadow of a sapper's body cut the lights of Kontum City. He pops a flare and sees the perimeter wire filled with the figures of enemy soldiers.

The firefight erupts. Our line opens with rifles and machine gun. Our mortars begin to send up flares that descend in their chutes, casting an eeriness to the fight. The Montagnards from A Company arrive at the bunkers and fire rifles and grenades into the attack.

Our mortars begin to fire HE and white phosphorous on the line just as the Communist regulars charge. Enemy bodies hang in the concertina wire like those tent caterpillar worms hang in the trees in clumps. They hang limp and black.

"Crispy critters!" I hear someone shout over the battle noise.

Then the enemy begins to rocket our camp from the hills.

One of our buildings takes a hit and begins to glow as it catches fire inside. Loose papers flutter in the air like lost white birds.

The attack begins to fail. Incoming fire is diminishing. The wave of troops that charged the camp and are alive are withdrawing, walking backward and firing at us. The sappers in the wire who are still alive cannot stand and flee, meet their end there.

The rain stops as suddenly as it began. We call in air support and the fast movers and gunships keep the perimeter lit up until daylight. The jets make napalm and gun runs all the way to the tree line.

It is Friday morning. Along the complex, enemy soldiers still hang in the wire, their bodies burned cinder black. Our building still smolders. Our seriously wounded lie on stretchers and wait for medevac.

Outside the wire in the morning fields, brown cattle feed on the wet grass. They are calm and chew contentedly without hurry. I can hear them as their teeth pull the grass from the soil. Their tails sweep back and forth across their flanks. A red sunrise is reflected in the remains of last night's rain. The puddles are blood red.

Haiku—Flowers in the Grass

Battlefields lie still
A dying sun hemorrhaged
On a cotton cloud

Humid and heavy
Even the air is sweating
As we leave the plane

Above the sea grass
Hooded cobra turns its head
Deadly periscope

Dale Hanson

War news — newspaper
Stuck fast on the wet sidewalk
Writhing in the wind

Bodiless fatigues
Dry on the concertina
Missing in action

Haiku—Flowers in the Grass

A pant leg and boot
Hang in the concertina
For illiterates

After the firefight
The taste of blood in my mouth
I'm able to taste

Heavily armed troops
Pause as they move on the trail
To let a snake pass

Dale Hanson

Water buffalo
Moves confidently onward
A child on its back

Kontum shopkeepers —
A storefront window displays
Dentures with black teeth

Painted grave markers
Behind them Vietnamese
Squat, then move along

Haiku—Flowers in the Grass

Tribesmen with their catch —
A live deer hangs from a pole
I avoid its eyes

(Sun)
Leaves — the village bonze
Hands to eyes disciples watch
Standing saffron robed

Frosty highlands night
I wrap my waterproof tarp
Over my rifle

Virgin Islands

Dale Hanson

The Caribbean
Painted houses and clothing —
Colors of parrots

A hairless gecko
Takes his place on my mirror
And watches me shave

Along the roadside
The leaves and flowers are trimmed
The height of donkeys

Haiku—Flowers in the Grass

Dust of the desert
Just arrived from Africa
Settles on my shoes

My sea turtle find
Seems so unimpressed with me
Merely blinks his eyes

In stolen shells, crabs
Roll themselves down the hillside
To make their escape

Dale Hanson

Hibiscus in mouth,
An iguana wiggles by —
Her name is Nancy

Songbirds weave their nests
Suspended from thin branches
Over the roadway

Waiting for darkness
Tree frogs passing themselves off
For singing thrushes

Haiku—Flowers in the Grass

Graceless pelicans
Drop from the sky in loud splats
Pouches full of fish

Pelicans on posts
Watch my feeble cast for fish
Eyes full of disgust

Dale Hanson

Hurricane's approach
Mangroves fiercely clutch the mud
With long black fingers

A nondescript goat
Tenderly her kid suckles
As any mother

SPRING

Dale Hanson

Rolled up snow fences
Lying along the roadside
Weary from winter

Sunrise, daffodils
Open their purses to glean
The gold of the day

The hut door opens
Both cat and a square of light
Let out in the night

Haiku—Flowers in the Grass

Sounds of fireflies —
Closing lids of mason jars
And laughing children

Crushed by my rude feat
Flowers grant me as I pause,
Fragrant forgiveness

Dale Hanson

Down the asphalt road
The youth imagines the world
Beyond the heat waves

Hear the lungs of spring
Calling of crows and children
With unchanged voices

Sweating glass jars hold
Forgotten black bugs that were
Last night's fireflies

Haiku—Flowers in the Grass

Like yellow finches
In my water-filled tulips
There are moons drinking

Panting butterfly
Resting on a rose bush thorn
This blustery day

Bare, wet, gnarled branches
Viewed before the street lights are
Changed into halos

Dale Hanson

Concentric circles
Where the water bug has stopped
A target for trout

Something jumps in a
Pond. A heron searches, but
Silence swallowed it.

Across the street I
Watch the blind lady as she
Weeds in her garden

Haiku—Flowers in the Grass

Shy moon on the pond
See her there hiding in the
Yellow lily pads

That sexy lady
Dragonfly is on the town
With her see-through wings

Dale Hanson

Columbine peering
Through the fence slats of the yard
Of the baseball field

Children gaze skyward
Their thoughts attached to the clouds
That are moving on

Haiku—Flowers in the Grass

Cupped in slim fingers
Of budding amaryllis
Are poised butterflies

"Spring forward, fall back"
Frightened in the empty church —
I missed the rapture!

Like scattered feathers
From a cat kill lie my rain-
Pounced tulip petals

Dale Hanson

Freed from its cocoon
A yellow butterfly lies
Panting in the sun

Intently watching
Is a thrush — a bead of dew
Rolling on a leaf

Spring offers a toast
Of rain-filled tulips beaded
With dew on the sides

Haiku—Flowers in the Grass

Trout just break surface
Of my pond perhaps to catch
Reflected blossoms

Tulips tip their spears
Toward the sun in salute
From their silent ranks

Dale Hanson

Ravens chide an owl
All perched in a single tree
In all the forest

Powdered butterflies
Go home bearing colors of
Visited flowers

Flitting here and there
Never staying — butterfly
Seeking for beauty

Haiku—Flowers in the Grass

The stone garden frog
Suns after the morning rain
Changing its color

Holding the slim wrist
Of a graceful flower I
Draw it to my lips

My sweating workhorse
In plowing even carries
The sun on his back

Dale Hanson

The salesgirl exits
For a time her perfume rides
In the taxi seat

Car tracks on this side
Car tracks emerge on that side
Muddy stream between

Haiku—Flowers in the Grass

Just for fun I move
'til the moon seems to settle
Into the bird's nest

Puddle in the road —
In it a bird takes a bath —
A road less traveled

Sitting on his heels
A child examines a bug
All else forgotten

Dale Hanson

A youthful spring sun
Has melted my winter path
To last fall's footprints

My nocturnal stroll —
Under the moon every moth
Appears beautiful

Moon, with pale fingers
Weaves branches into a net
Which captures itself

Haiku—Flowers in the Grass

Low tide — with a stick
A girl writes in the wet sand
"Love you forever"

Bird cacophony
Innkeeper's hoe scraping nests
From under the eaves

Dale Hanson

A child's first horror
Below the nest, ants swarming
On a naked bird

Folded into buds
Origami touched by rain
Unfolding itself

Haiku—Flowers in the Grass

Dusk with her basket
Takes the colors of the day
And leaves all the rest

Around the yard light
Flying bats and children play
With high pitched voices

Lovers count the swans
That reside in the flats —
An even number!

Dale Hanson

Marsh flowers just picked
Collapse before we get home
Life drained from their stems

Spring rain, dark wet woods
Laughing children emerging
Arms full of cowslips

Haiku—Flowers in the Grass

Too poor for perfume
Country girl meets her boyfriend
Under a lilac tree

SUMMER

Dale Hanson

Birds flit in the trees
A dislodged drop of old rain
Lands on my forehead

Indecisive breeze —
Plays with a paper cup like
A cat with a mouse

Grandma rings her hands
Watching lightning from the car
"Safe on rubber tires!"

Haiku—Flowers in the Grass

Where life places it
Bamboo clings with grasping hands
All knuckles and joints

In the dentist chair
Scenic prints on the ceiling
Wishing I were there

Returning trollers
Poke through the fog. Sleek needles
Pulling lines of thread

Dale Hanson

Ringing in the fog —
The bell on the channel buoy
Same tone as the church

In my sleep I swat
The buzzing alarm clock like
A persistent fly

Haiku—Flowers in the Grass

Caught on the sidewalk
Slugs melt as they flee before
A hot pursuing sun

Ants, all wet with dew
Working at a common goal
Each carries the sun

Exhausted, the sun
At the end of the day lies
Upon the still lake

Dale Hanson

Waving toward me
Even hermits seem friendly
Swatting mosquitoes

Jigging for herring
The dock glitters with fish scales
Fathers and children

The fallen leaves float
Drifting slowly down a stream
For a cricket's boat

Haiku—Flowers in the Grass

Tipping in the wind,
Swallows cling to the wires
Like wooden clothes pins

The parchment of sky
That records today is done,
Yellowed in the sun

Dale Hanson

As if with one foot
On the ground, the wind jostles
Empty schoolyard swings

The honeybees fan
Their dry paper house — see them
Darting yellow flames

Open billed skimmers
Slice a page of calm water
Avian scissors

Haiku—Flowers in the Grass

The moon is gliding
Nocturnal moths to trysts with
Scentless white flowers

Crazily my kite
Struggles against the thin string
That has lent it life

Lazy hitchhiker
Fog sits astride the river
As it moves along

Dale Hanson

Clusters of berries
Break apart in the morning
Into lady bugs

On the path — a slug
Same direction that I go
Fellow traveler

A hot summer day
Just the scarecrow holds a rake
As we swim the lake

Haiku—Flowers in the Grass

Parking lot, light rain,
Departing automobiles
Leaving their shadows

Night and partial moon
Edgecumbe's snow-capped peak
Suspended in sky

Dale Hanson

In yellow and red
Scarves wrapped around their round heads
Are berry pickers

A cancelled picnic
The dip in the horseshoe pit
Fills up with water

Fields of sunflowers
All appear to stare at me
Sun at my back

Haiku—Flowers in the Grass

A heavy downpour —
In the bus stop the stray dog
And I are comrades

A hot summer porch
Two hairy-legged grasshoppers
Spitting tobacco

Dale Hanson

With dignified step
Raven scrapes gum from the walk
With his long sharp beak

Soviet paintings
Laughing peasants with faces
Like polished apples

Evening in the house
On the window ledge the cat
Lies next to herself

Haiku—Flowers in the Grass

Sitting thoughtfully
Small frogs, so small on the shore,
Smiling at Pharaoh

Drunkard's walk home
Butterfly follows beside
Matches flight to step

Tapping with his cane
The blind man passes my bench —
Seems angry today!

Dale Hanson

Ducks in summer skies
Each flies low to its own place
None in formation

His porch light is on.
I stop at the blind man's house
To see an old friend

On the path I walk
Sparrow's delicate footprints
Set in the cement

Haiku—Flowers in the Grass

Crumpled paper bags
Roll across the road — wind blown
Running brown rabbits

Frog's chest is hairless
With skinny arms at his side
Still king of his pond

Philosopher frog
Leaps from the log in the pond
Jumps into himself

Dale Hanson

Only the darkness
Of the pit itself kept my
Shadow from falling in

AUTUMN

Dale Hanson

Bachelor scarecrow
No chance outside the farmhouse
Dressed in hand-me-downs

Workday's end — both hands,
Exhausted, hang limply down
Inside of the clock

A cold north wind blows —
Near the harbor lily pads
Pull at their anchors

Haiku—Flowers in the Grass

"Class of '65"
Painted on rocks and faded
And covered with moss

Low tide — salmon hang
Exposed in set nets and wait
Judgment of the day

Dale Hanson

Sibilant frog is
Waiting on his umbrella
For October rain

The crow I despise —
He stole the bright bottle caps
From my scarecrow's eyes

October playmates —
The wind and laughing children
Chasing the same leaves

Haiku—Flowers in the Grass

Wading the cold stream
My faithful reflection feels
Compelled to shiver

The wind blows away
The words I say on our walk
And whispers its own

Getting a new dog —
I gauge its expected years
With those of my own

Dale Hanson

First rain drops — ice cold
Drop suddenly on the trees
The leaves seem to flinch

August rainforest
Just the caw of the raven
Has escaped the rain

Haiku—Flowers in the Grass

Last leaf drops away
In the tree at forest edge
Only an owl remains

The moon's pale skin is
Veined by willow branches that
Shiver in the night

Old jack-o-lantern
Saved for the scarecrow's new head
Fierce enough by spring

Dale Hanson

Mid October winds —
Canary flocks set to flight
By calico cats

Where did summer go?
Sadly, I see an old man
Dig gladioli

Haiku—Flowers in the Grass

Maple leaves shiver
Like those Russian newsreel crowds
Waving red banners

Prosperous harvest
More than enough husks to make
Another scarecrow

Orchard stroll, cloud burst.
Bald head to the rain I fill
My hat with cherries

Dale Hanson

Just so in the light
I see myself reflected
In my old dog's eyes

Some consolation!
My old crippled dog, now deaf,
Doesn't fear thunder.

Haiku—Flowers in the Grass

In my path ahead
Windblown leaves scurry across
Like small brown lemmings

All this sleepless night
A lonely cricket has searched
My pile of dry leaves

Tossed jack-o-lanterns —
The carved smiles soften and sag,
Collapse into frowns

Dale Hanson

On a paper-white
Page of water, lines of geese
Swim by in sentences

Night frost, morning sun
The roof of the fire hall
Flaming tongues of steam

The old, near-blind dog
Once again barks at scarecrow
Who yet stands his ground

Haiku—Flowers in the Grass

Fall casts its shadow
Below poplars and birch trees
In yellow and red

The farmer's wife smiles —
In her sleep she hears the last
Canning jar lid seal

Dale Hanson

Canning jar lids pop
The farmer's wife is counting
Even in her sleep

Even scarecrow dies —
On a day, dead calm, he falls
Snapping of old sticks

Scales — color of corn
The old barn snake ends its night
Coiled on a grain sack

Haiku—Flowers in the Grass

Autumn, shifting winds
Brown leaves in the tennis court
Racing side to side

Boats moored side by side
Gossip about their ailments
Creaking harbor boats

Dale Hanson

Empty little town
Even the geese are leaving
At the harvest's end

After stealing corn
The tramp compares scarecrow's clothes
With those of his own

Under harvest moon
Tombstones shine white in the dark
As we hurry by

Haiku—Flowers in the Grass

Strength of youth now gone,
The old man's back just carries
A sliver of moon

Last maple leaves cling —
Five brown fingers still clutching
And veins on their backs

Sun shines on the wall
Leaving a shadow of frost
Where the bike had been

Dale Hanson

Dusk and nearly dark
The scene's details fade away
Only the swans remain

Night sits on haunches
Brown leaves rustle on the walk
A cat's eye of moon

HAIKU—FLOWERS IN THE GRASS

There, frozen mid-step
Drunk in the graveyard sees fog
Rising from the tombstones

Winter

Dale Hanson

Fishing trips, long past —
Even the memories now
Are catch and release

The much used straw broom
Bent just to match the bow of
The housekeeper's back

Newspaper headlines
Fixed in a puddle, blowing,
Disintegrating

Haiku—Flowers in the Grass

(Melted Snowman)
Lying at the door
Boots, gloves, hats and melting snow
With nothing between

Pick up day. Trash cans
Line snow filled streets left and right
An urban punch card

White owls drop from boughs
Which are laden with snowfall
Then utter silence

Dale Hanson

Dead cold. A squirrel
Peels layers of sound that were
Frozen in pine cones

Field mice hesitate
Passing fence posts where snow seems
Poised on its haunches

Haiku—Flowers in the Grass

Thousands of starlings
Roosting in every branch
Winter foliage

Winter armistice
Blackbirds are picking the corn
From the scarecrow's pipe

Square fields of new snow
As yet unwritten on by
The feet of poets

Dale Hanson

Winter photographs
Waterfalls, frozen and mute
Framed within the rock

Through the window, sun
Places its yellow blanket
On the sleepy dog

Falling, the snow paints
Our house in white, water black,
And the village lights pink

Haiku—Flowers in the Grass

The defroster on —
Paper slips on the dash are
Fluttering to life

From fields now snow filled
Even the faithful scarecrows
Have left for winter

Dale Hanson

The field lies covered
With a sheet of snow that is
Being stitched by deer

Slowly the sun drops.
Shadows of hungry branches
Reach across the snow

Haiku—Flowers in the Grass

The moon holds the light
As the breeze untangles the fog
Caught in bare branches

Oh Me! Stags in snow
Too soon departing — their prints
Are cups of shadow

Approaching midday
The sun shrinks the arrogance
Of morning shadow

Dale Hanson

A prairie snowstorm—
Shutters of empty houses
Slap their sides for warmth

Stuffed with stocks of grain
My scarecrow but attracts them
This cold winter day

Haiku—Flowers in the Grass

Putting on my pants
As I watch the Olympics —
My own balance beam

Winter and ice cold
An old man with brittle steps
Walks into the night

Bright northern lights flare
Distant Eskimos whistle
To make them brighter

Dale Hanson

Ice cold winter day
Chimney smoke from a snug cabin
Reluctant to leave

Deepening snow drifts
Through them are tracks of tall moose
And weightless field mice

Grouse dive into drifts —
Along the crests are fox tracks
Connecting the dots

Haiku—Flowers in the Grass

A polar bear stalks
One paw covers his black nose
Near a wary seal

Sifting of snow drifts
Northern lights sway in the sky
Rustle of curtains

Northern lights, all night
Stuck on a constellation.
Snow drifts through the trees.

Dale Hanson

Totem Park snow fall
The bare shoulders of the frog
Are also covered

Under the street light
Snow ventures on the ice
Among the skaters

HAIKU—FLOWERS IN THE GRASS

Snowflakes fall, flitting
Drifting here and there seeking
The right place to land

Heavy falling snow
Seems people and ravens too
Speak through wool mittens

In cracks in the rocks
Water settles for winter
Flexes its shoulders

Dale Hanson

Tide pools freezing in —
Only one remains open —
A heron is in it

Old folks at the home
Pausing at the waxed hallway
Rubber tipped crutches

Empty skating rink
Wisps of snow swirl on the ice
The moon for a light

Haiku—Flowers in the Grass

At the old man's house
His forgotten flowerpots
Are filling with snow

Huge white flakes of snow
Descend slowly on the fields
Swans call in the night

So bow-legged tonight
Eskimo on pressure ice
The moon on his back

Dale Hanson

Ice fishing all day
Norwegian hasn't moved once
Perhaps I should check

A gale from Russia
A storm that batters the shore
And straightens the flag

Outside the diner
Snowflakes sizzle on the hood
Of my just parked car

For All Seasons

Dale Hanson

The wind on the pond
Breaks the moon in pieces, then
Leaves it assembled

Orphan gnat alights
On the cathedral window
With wings of stained glass

The widow cried out
"Thieves are in the attic!" as
Crows grub on her roof

Haiku—Flowers in the Grass

Distant plane departs.
Engine sounds chasing after.
Tardy passenger.

Empty water tank
On its lid struts a raven —
Such important feet

Through the cell window
Even the sun on the floor
Appears there in bars

Dale Hanson

Soaked through in the rain
The drunkard no longer seeks
A dry place to sit

At my window sill
Canaries cock their heads — sing
With my new tea pot

Sunrise casts yellow
Beams through the dark forest as
From lighted windows

Haiku—Flowers in the Grass

The elevator doors
Open-close, open and close
Swallowing people

Fog. Boats pass like hands
That disappear into sleeves
Of a kimono

Dale Hanson

The village drunkard
Walks home, his journey traced by
House lights in their turn

Fishing boats are moored
Side to side — accordions —
And played by the sea

Just now abandoned
For a new toy, the balloon
Follows my child's wake

Haiku—Flowers in the Grass

Butterflies spotted
On the hillside signaling
With their semaphores

On my cracked window
A puzzled spider ventures
Across the smooth web

Beneath an ancient tree
With limbs in blossom reads a
Samurai haiku

Dale Hanson

Who waits for God's sun?
Butterflies laden with dew
Too heavy to fly

Shorebird vanity
Peering into each tide pool
Looking at themselves

Haiku—Flowers in the Grass

Through the holy place
Priests dare not go — A bug walks —
No soul and no sin

Wind tosses her hair —
With a cart full of blossoms
A child hurries home

Dale Hanson

Through the cell window
Shadows pass across the walk
From unseen birds

Through buttercups walked
A bear — around a raised paw
Behold: honeybees!

Haiku—Flowers in the Grass

On African plains
See them — the Lord's fingerprints
In shapes of horses

Long hard winter's end
Snow fences rolled in bundles
All with ribs exposed

Thought empty at dusk
Unknowingly a spider
Captured the spectrum

Dale Hanson

The hem of fog's robe
Catches fast on Mount Edgecumbe
Breaks free in tatters

To crumbs magpies fly
Black and white, black and white then
Leave iridescent

Down the railroad tracks
Steel rails turning into heat waves
Distant train whistle

Haiku—Flowers in the Grass

Lady spider threads
A necklace of diamonds
Made of stolen dew

An abandoned farm —
On the dry well taunting — a
Dusty drinking cup

Blowflies on entrails
So unafraid of lions
On this slain zebra

Dale Hanson

Thin pencils of fog
Are erasing the mountains
Of Sitka's landscape

Companion moon is
Casting his net in the wake
Of my fishing boat

Testing an old well
The dropped stone ends in a thud
Echoes of my heart

Haiku—Flowers in the Grass

Knowing exactly
The length of the yard dog's rope
The cat struts about

Nervously chickens
Edge to the coop — I had been
Thoughtless with my kite

Dale Hanson

Rapping woodpecker
Commanding authority
At the hollow tree

Gulls and sandpipers
Vain runners of the tide flat
Peering in each pool

Turning on one wing
Placing it upon nothing
Before empty sky

Haiku—Flowers in the Grass

Small consolation.
In the darkness the lion,
Like me, has a cough

A nervous light wind
Caused the wild iris stocks to
Twitch like waiting lions

Dale Hanson

Her evening done,
She sets out her lace to dry
Off the dew — a spider

First rain drops on my
Dry walk bear to my nostrils
The smell of road dust

A palace guardsman
Bars the entrance — across his
Forehead walks — a fly

Haiku—Flowers in the Grass

A hint of an eye
Behind a thin lid of cloud
In this sleepy night

Outside — a storm swell
In harbor — see the breathing
Of boats in their births

Vanished butterflies
My eyes lost them to a field
Of blowing daisies

Dale Hanson

This sleepy morning
Even my coffee maker's
Perking seems to snore

First robin arrives
Braving this last of winter
Wearing its sweater

Even in rain, mud
Puddles reflect the sky, now
Disintegrating

Haiku—Flowers in the Grass

Roman Coliseum
The color of ancient blood
As I pass it by

Betrayed — the panther's
Stealthy prowl follows a wake
Of silence of frogs

Dale Hanson

Fish scraps tossed to sea
Materialize into
Graceful sea lions

Do not tease me, wren.
Old friend, I know that you but
Sing for strawberries

Haiku—Flowers in the Grass

Ahah! A song sheet —
Power lines against white sky
With sparrows for notes

Beelzebub's children
Guilt ridden flies forever
Washing their slim hands

Camouflaged fruit flies
Dine in my sandwich bag dressed
In cellophane wings

Dale Hanson

Daylight, in leaving,
Gathered all her belongings
From the darkened room

Shaking lupine seeds
Into a folded paper
Old gold rush cabin

The girl in patches
Chooses and hugs as her own
A tossed-away doll

Haiku—Flowers in the Grass

An African sun —
In baobab trees even
Lions are melting

Ancient totem pole
Wood grain raised over the years
Shaman's wrinkled face

In the dark near shore
The breathing of sleeping whales
Then utter silence

Dale Hanson

On the power lines
Birds the color of cinders
Wings and tails twitching

Cat like, darkness slips
To my bird bath and laps it
Until it is gone

My lanky grandson
Exits the car — arms and legs
Unfolding himself

Haiku—Flowers in the Grass

Ancient priest's gnarled hands —
Strings of fingers intertwined
Round knuckles for beads

My gentle pond seems
To reach upward to catch a
Struggling falling leaf

Dale Hanson

A gust on the pond
Sliver of reflected moon
Broken to pieces

The night tipped her pail
Of blossoms spilling petals
Splashing my garden

A fist of hard stone
Releases the dew of night
To the morning sun

Haiku—Flowers in the Grass

The mountain gathers
Silken threads of fog to spin
Into a cocoon

Fog horns from the boats
Old captains picking their way
By echoes from shore

Departing, the sun
Lights candles on the decks of
Lilly pads in bloom

Dale Hanson

Dumping sour milk
The open-mouthed container
Gulping for fresh air

An afternoon game
The sun tempts the dog to lie
In its square, then moves

Bespeckled pigeons
Stroll across the courthouse lawn
Hands behind their backs

HAIKU—FLOWERS IN THE GRASS

Hospital quiet
Excited deaf visitors
Signing through the glass

Morning — still as glass
A heron walks on tip toe
So not to break it

From his cell he turns
Hollyhocks by reflecting
The sun with his cup

Dale Hanson

Fog and rain surround
Sitka like a cocoon on
One grey branch of road

Twilight — a full day
Against the lake all my friends
Become silhouettes

Moslem call to prayer
One musical note being
Circled by a bee

Haiku—Flowers in the Grass

On the power lines
Birds roost — ones and twos — Morse code
For a slow reader

Child student in awe
School janitor's raw power
In his rings of keys

Dale Hanson

An accusing moon
Lighting the hands of a thief
Lurking in a thicket

Emerald glaciers
At the sea present themselves
For an offering

Haiku—Flowers in the Grass

A jet is pulling
A yellow zipper across
A clear linen sky

The hand of the storm
Covers the eye of the moon
Before its fury

Swell chested spring streams
Like tailors are hemming the
White skirts of winter

Dale Hanson

An overdue bill
Crumpled into a tight ball
Unfolding itself

Fish shaped kite and tail
Swims upward into blue sky
Against the current

Nurses — all in white
Hustle down hospital halls —
Human corpuscles

Haiku—Flowers in the Grass

Blown free of the web
An empty carapace slides
Along the sidewalk

Following the tide
In virgin sand even feet
Make fleeting halos

Doll in a glass case
Perfect in her frilly dress
Inapproachable

Dale Hanson

Too few flowers, she
Adds their shadows to the wall
To fill the bouquet

The chef spies a duck —
A paprika colored head,
Its bill like ginger

Haiku—Flowers in the Grass

There at the roadside,
Fingers curled in a gesture,
Lies an empty glove

Sparrows are bathing
In the water-filled footprints
Of yesterday's bear

Kayaks passing by
Dipping sunlight from the sea
With their paddle blades

Dale Hanson

Rainfall from the coast —
Each drop carries on its back
The scent of the sea

Sun points its finger
To whales in the far distance
Spouts of liquid light

Chased by a red fox
A mouse seeks refuge in the
Shadow of a bear

Haiku—Flowers in the Grass

Storm surge in the harbor
Mooring lines of tethered boats
Groaning with the strain

Empty prairie shack
Inhospitable for guests
Door sagged tightly shut

(Owl)
A piece of grey fog
Drops down — gone, leaving behind
Thin feathers of mist

Dale Hanson

Cheese colored sunlight
Lies on the dining table
Sliced by window blinds

His evening walk —
The blind man takes his lantern
So none trip on him

Frenzied gulls descend
Their image on the sea change
To spawning herring

Haiku—Flowers in the Grass

Through the window slats
Sun laying stripes on the cat
Who dreams of tigers

Two nesting sparrows
Fetch twigs dropped in winter storms
Returned to the tree

Heard clearly and far
Not the most beautiful but —
The bell most empty

Dale Hanson

Purse seiners fishing
Drawing in their nets to close
Squeezing out seagulls

Middle of the night
Traffic light still directing
In the empty streets

Its voice sounds clearly
Through the village, the old bell
Empty of itself

Haiku—Flowers in the Grass

Freeze, thaw, freeze and thaw
Spring is squeezing water from
White sponges of snow.

Ice cold — nothing moves
Even Basho's frog is gone
Frozen in the mud

Barnyard animals
Necks stretched through the pasture fence
Flowers in the grass

ABOUT THE AUTHOR

Dale Hanson is an accomplished sculptor who has led a life of adventure and enjoyed numerous accomplishments. He is a black belt martial artist, an author, a pilot of fixed wing and glider airplanes, has flown aerobatics and is a Special Forces underwater diver. He is a disabled veteran and a member of MENSA.

During the Vietnam War, Dale was a highly decorated Green Beret who served three years as a commando in the famous SOG program, whose mission involved extremely dangerous raids far behind enemy lines. This unit received more decorations and suffered higher rates of casualties than any American unit since the American Civil

Dale Hanson

War. On one of these raids, Dale earned the first of several purple hearts as his right hand was mangled by a burst of machine gun fire. It is ironic that he became a sculptor, a field in which one's hands are so critical.

The artistic fruit of those hands today can be found in collections of thousands of people throughout the world. Signature to his work is a strong emphasis on artistic composition, grace, and flowing lines, combined with attention to detail.

In haiku, Dale has expressed his artistic talent in perhaps the most disciplined of written forms. With great economy of words, the writer of haiku is challenged to express concepts and insight as seen in everyday observations. In his work, Dale skillfully points out from the commonplace that which one may have missed and then makes application to life.